J
EDWARDS, R
If only..

7 SEP 1994

15 DEC 1994

27 JAN 1995

8 MAR 1995

IF ONLY...

Richard Edwards

IF ONLY...

Illustrated by Alison Claire Darke

VIKING KESTREL

VIKING KESTREL

Published by the Penguin Group
27 Wrights Lane, London W8 5TZ, England
Viking Penguin Inc., 40 West 23rd Street, New York, New York 10010, USA
Penguin Books Australia Ltd, Ringwood, Victoria, Australia
Penguin Books Canada Ltd, 2801 John Street, Markham, Ontario, Canada L3R 1B4
Penguin Books (NZ) Ltd, 182–190 Wairau Road, Auckland 10, New Zealand

Penguin Books Ltd, Registered Offices: Harmondsworth, Middlesex, England

First published 1990
1 3 5 7 9 10 8 6 4 2

Text copyright © Richard Edwards, 1990
Illustrations copyright © Alison Claire Darke, 1990

All rights reserved. Without limiting the rights under copyright reserved above,
no part of this publication may be reproduced, stored in or introduced into a
retrieval system, or transmitted, in any form or by any means (electronic,
mechanical, photocopying, recording or otherwise), without the prior written
permission of both the copyright owner and the above publisher of this book

Filmset in Linotron Palatino by
Rowland Phototypesetting (London) Ltd

Printed in Great Britain by
Butler & Tanner, Frome and London

A CIP catalogue record for this book is available from the British Library

ISBN 0–670–82559–X

Contents

Chef	7
Knight	9
Gardener	10
Pilot	12
Waiter	15
Astronomer	17
Statue	18
Snowman	20
Ghost	23
Mermaid	24
Zookeeper	27
Castaway	29
Architect	31
Pirate	33
Angel	34
Father Christmas	37
Artist	38
Explorer	40
Shoemaker	43
Archaeologist	45
Conductor	46
Traindriver	48
Barber	51
Mountaineer	52
Scarecrow	55
Shepherd	56
Shipwrecked	58
Acrobat	61
Shopkeeper	63

If only I could be a chef –
A posh one with a hat on –
I'd make huge omelettes, giant puddings,
Pies that could be sat on,
Pork sausages as long as logs
With shovel-loads of mustard,
A jelly like a mountainside
And Norfolk Broads of custard.

If I wore shining armour
Like knights of long ago,
I'd ride out after breakfast,
Cross streams, cross fields of snow,
Climb wild enchanted mountains,
Chop off a dragon's head,
Ride home through wolf-filled forests
And be back in time for bed.

If I could be a gardener
I'd plant unusual things:
Boiled eggplants and horse-chestnut trees
With conkers tied to strings,
A dog-rose with a waggly tail,
A gooseberry with feathers
And sunflowers wearing raincoats
For the worst of English weathers.

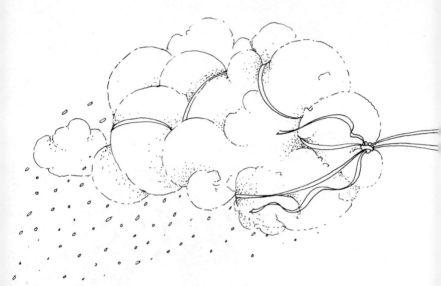

If I could be a pilot
Each Christmas Eve I'd fly
To fetch a fluffy snow cloud
From the distant Arctic sky,
I'd chase it, catch it, tow it home
And tie it to a tree,
So snow would fall on Christmas Day
On all my friends and me.

If I worked in a restaurant
And customers were rude,
I'd 'accidentally' trip as I
Was serving them their food,
So some would get a soup shampoo
And some a gravy eyeful,
And, oh, what sweet revenge I'd have
With bowls of sloppy trifle!

If I were an astronomer
I'd scan the skies all night,
Till, through my great big telescope,
A planet spun in sight,
A planet full of bug-eyed men,
As green as green could be,
Who, through their great big telescopes,
Stared goggling back at me.

If I could be a statue
I'd stand in Nelson's place
And gaze out over London
With a smiling stony face,
But if the pigeons came too close
I'd shout and I'd stamp and I'd scare
The birds, the lions and all of the tourists
Out of Trafalgar Square.

If I were made of snow and ice
I'd hold a New Year's spree,
Inviting all my frosty friends
To jive and jamboree,
Sing 'Auld Lang Syne' then hokey-cokey
Under midnight skies,
While children at their bedroom windows
Blinked and rubbed their eyes.

If I went 'Ooooo!' and wore a sheet
I'd haunt the corridors
Of some old Scottish country house
With draughts and creaky floors,
And when the guests sat down to dine
I'd float out, pale and shrieky,
To scare them from their haggises
And steamy cock-a-leekie.

If I could breathe beneath the sea,
Half person and half fish,
I'd dive down till I found a coral door
And in I'd swish
To swim through weedy canyons
And find the hall of stone
Where Neptune rules the oceans
From his dolphin-guarded throne.

If only, with a bunch of keys,
I kept a private zoo,
I wouldn't capture elephants
Or cage a cockatoo,
I'd lock away Prime Ministers
To read their dusty speeches,
While passing bears and chimpanzees
Threw buns and rotten peaches.

If I lived on a desert island,
Just me and the waves
And palms and sand and coconuts
And sun and coves and caves,
I'd sometimes fish or hunt or swim
Or ride my goat called Crusoe,
Or, if I felt like dozing off,
Just lie right down and do so.

If I could be an architect
I'd draw up new designs
With ears and tails and curly bits,
Not angles, corners, lines,
And then, instead of boring flats
And houses shaped like boxes,
We'd live in brick sheep, tiger towns
And rows of terraced foxes.

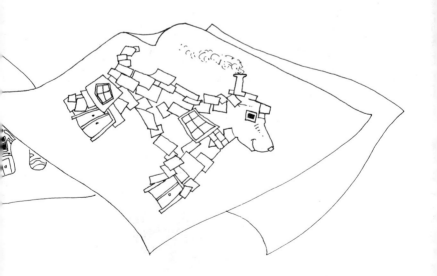

If only I were blacker-hearted,
Never seasick, bolder,
I'd be a daring pirate
With a parrot on my shoulder,
I'd ambush Spanish galleons
And pinch their treasure trove,
And bury gold on every beach
From Zanzibar to Hove.

If I became an angel
I'd throw away my harp
And thump a drum or toot a hooter –
Clatter! Bang! Parp-parp!
I'd drift about kazooing
With cymbals in my hand
Till all the saints were rocking
To my one-man angel band.

If I were Father Christmas
I'd deliver all my toys
By rocket ship, a sleigh's too slow
For eager girls and boys,
I'd nip down every chimney-pot
And never miss a roof,
While Rudolf worked the ship's controls
With antler tip and hoof.

If I could paint I'd walk round town,
Colouring dull things bright:
All churches green, all lampposts gold,
All pavements red and white,
And if the sky turned gloomy,
Then as fast as you could blink,
I'd draw a ladder, climb up quick
And splosh the grey clouds pink.

If I were an explorer
I'd reach that far-off land
Called Jumbledup, where sand was sea
And sea was made of sand,
Where snow fell every summer
On herds of grazing bees,
And cows flew round the blossom
Of the orange apple trees.

If I made shoes, they wouldn't be
Ordinary, run of the mill,
I'd make some pairs with clockwork wheels
To help you up a hill,
And some with wings and some with horns
That beeped in crowded places,
And some that made you vanish when
You twiddled with their laces.

If, in some stony desert place,
I dug deep underground,
I'd reach a sealed Egyptian tomb
That no one else had found
And, wriggling in, I'd gaze on sights
Five thousand quiet years old:
A Pharaoh and his mummy wrapped
In sheets of burning gold.

If I were the conductor
Of an orchestra I'd choose
Piano-playing monkeys
And, as cellists, kangaroos,
A hippo on the piccolo,
A sloth on xylophone
And one giant, eight-legged octopus
Who'd play four flutes alone.

If only I could drive a train
I'd fit it with computers
And take off on a mystery tour
To startle bored commuters,
And how they'd gaze and mutter
As we flew between the stars
To pull in, only two hours late,
At platform four on Mars.

If I had shiny scissors
And I owned a barber's shop,
I'd snip all day till five and even then
I wouldn't stop,
I'd walk home trimming hedges
And lawns and dogs and cats,
And woe betide all grans who passed
With feathers in their hats!

If I could be a mountaineer
I'd trek into the heart
Of unknown Himalayan hills
Where glassy glaciers start,
And over minestrone soup
And bowls of warm spaghetti
I'd while away the chilly evenings
Chatting with the Yeti.

If I were made of sticks and straw
And clothes tied on with string,
I wouldn't frighten birds away –
I'd wave them down to sing.
All day I'd sway to cheeps and tweets
And every night I'd swoon
To nightingale serenades
Beneath the rising moon.

If I could be a shepherd
I'd teach my baaing flocks
To knit and turn out fleecy vests
And pullovers and socks,
So when the winter blizzards
Stormed through the hills like bullies,
My sheep would simply smile, wrapped up
In home-made winter woollies.

If I were shipwrecked on a plank –
No boat, no food, no hope –
I'd call a flock of pigeons
And I'd throw them up a rope,
And as they hauled me back to shore,
Wings straining with their load,
I'd sigh and thank my lucky stars
For being pigeon-towed.

If I could bounce and leap and be
A tumbling acrobat,
I'd never go in ferry boats or trains
Or things like that,
I'd cartwheel down to Dover docks
And, with one daring prance,
Vault clean across the Channel
For spring holidays in France.

If only I could keep a shop
I'd fill my shelves with wares
That other shops don't ever sell
Like socks in single pairs,
Like beds for dormice, hats for cats,
Like snow and trickly streams,
Like jars of mud and bubbles and,
For children only, dreams.